TOXIC FALL

by

Doris Anne Beaulieu

Copyrights © 2025

All Rights Reserved

No part of this book may be reproduced or transmitted in any form or by any means, electronic or mechanical, including photocopying, recording, or by any information storage and retrieval system without the written permission of the author, except where permitted by law.

CAUTION

This book is for 18+ mature audiences. The goal is to bring awareness to what you write on the internet, as there are potential consequences to yourself and people exposed to it. It may trigger others to do harm. Releasing frustration or just getting things off your chest is good, but doing so may be better in person with a friend, not with strangers—for the world to see and read. If you are triggered by abuse, this is not the book for you. Please choose one of my other books.

TABLE OF CONTENTS

CAST & SETTINGS..7

ACT I 9

   SCENE I..3

   SCENE II...7

   SCENE III 10

   SCENE IV 16

   SCENE V 18

   SCENE VI 23

ACT II..27

   SCENE I..29

   SCENE II...32

   SCENE III 34

   SCENE IV 36

   SCENE V 41

   SCENE VI 43

   SCENE VII..48

   SCENE VIII 51

ACT III 57

SCENE I 59
SCENE II 63
SCENE III 66
SCENE IV 76
SCENE V 79
SCENE VI 85
SCENE VII 95
SCENE VIII 99
SCENE IX 105
SCENE X 116
SCENE XI 118

CAST & SETTINGS

MAIN CHARACTERS:

- DEBRA: The mother
- JOE: The father
- SUSAN: The 5-year-old daughter.
- ALLEY: The 3-year-old daughter

OTHER CHARACTERS:

- MRS. LISA CROW: Joe's mother
- TIM CROW: Joe's brother
- BARBARA: Debra's mother
- OFFICER HARPER
- OFFICER GORDON
- OFFICER BLISS

SUPPORTING CHARACTERS:

- MR.BATES: Criminal Lawyer
- JUDGE CORNAIL
- MISS JENNA DAVIS: Social Worker
- CHARLIE= Coast Guard
- PASTER BURKE
- DISPATCHER ELLEN
- DR. JONES

COMPUTER FRIENDS:

- TOM
- CAROL
- KEVIN
- JOHNATHAN
- JACKIE
- PAUL

SETTINGS

- DEBRA AND JOE'S HOUSE.
- CHATROOM DANCE HALL.
- BINGO HALL.
- DARK STREETS.
- HOSPITAL.
- JAIL.
- COURTROOM.
- JOE'S MOM'S HOUSE.
- FISHERMAN DOCK.

ACT I

SCENE I

INT: KITCHEN – EARLY EVENING

Debra is setting up the table for supper. Joe comes home and goes to wash his hands for supper as the girls go to take their seats at the table.

JOE	How was your day with the girls?
DEBRA	Fine! I took them for a walk down to the corner store for an ice cream before their nap.
	(continues)
	How was the fishing today?
JOE	I worked hard today. Our traps were full, so we had to work fast and hard. Not much time for lunch; we barely got time to even grab a bite between traps, so I'm hungry tonight. We stopped for a beer on the way home to catch our breath and wind down from the rush of the day.
DEBRA	Joe, you shouldn't drink and drive.

JOE	Don't worry about my drinking. You like the paychecks just fine, don't you?
DEBRA	We're doing fine, dear.
JOE	You better believe it. I provide for my girls just fine.

(continues)

> You know, at the bar, a lady was crying that her husband just broke up and left her because he couldn't handle his three kids anymore. What a jerk!

Debra heads to the table and starts serving supper on the plates as Joe follows her.

DEBRA	Kind of like a guy in the chatroom today, saying his wife won't stay home to take care of their children when she doesn't work. He's working to pay the babysitter and feels his kids are being raised by the babysitter.
JOE	I wouldn't put up with that. What are you doing in chatrooms anyway?

At this point, Joe is cutting or trying to cut his steak. He throws his fork and knife on the table, barely missing his 3-year-old Alley, who jumps and starts crying. Then, he swings his plate at Debra.

The plate breaks, with chips falling all over the place, even in the girl's food and hair.

JOE That's tough as leather, you know I like it medium rare. I don't work hard to see you waste my money like this.

Joe is now standing. He's yelling and pointing at Debra while the girls freeze in place.

JOE You need to stay off the computer and pay attention to your cooking so I can have me a decent meal when I come home. Do I make myself clear?

Debra grabs the girls' plates and brushes their hair off to make sure no pieces of plate are still on them anywhere. She then sends them to the bathroom and puts all their clothes in the hamper, getting ready for a bath.

DEBRA Yes, Joe, I'm sorry.

JOE With the little bit of work you do around here all day, you should be able to get one thing right.

Joe walks to the refrigerator and grabs a beer then heads to the living room.

JOE (hollering) I'm hungry. Fix me a sandwich or something I can eat now!

DEBRA Yes, dear, coming.

Joe eats and drinks, watching Debra clean up around the table till he falls asleep in the recliner. Debra fixes the girls something to eat in their room and gets them to bed.

FADE OUT:

SCENE II

INT: KITCHEN-EARLY MORNING

Debra is getting the girls their cereal as Joe grabs his lunch and kisses the girls goodbye before he walks to the door.

FADE IN:

JOE	What are your plans for the day?
DEBRA	Just cleaning the house, then after the girls nap, I'll go do groceries.
JOE	Be home by the time I get home, and have my supper ready. Make sure you stay off the computer so my supper is edible this time.
DEBRA	Hopefully, the girls will take an early nap.
JOE	I'll need clean clothes for my night out with the guys tonight.

Debra cleans up behind the girls. She puts a load of clothes in the washer and off to the computer she goes.

DEBRA   Oh, gosh, girls! Time got away from me. Help Mama out and clean your room before Dad gets home while I fix something to eat.

SUSAN   (5-year-old daughter) Mom, you told Dad we were doing groceries today.

DEBRA   Go clean your room. I'll make you girls a sandwich, and you'll be able to nap on the way to the grocery store. Okay!

Susan comes running in the kitchen and hollers.

SUSAN   Mom, Alley (the three-year-old daughter) won't help me clean the room. Daddy will get mad again tonight.

DEBRA   You girls, come eat your sandwiches while I quickly clean your room. Now, eat fast!

Debra's eyes open wide as she walks into the bedroom. She sees the walls and floor are all marked up with markers. Debra talks to herself as she picks up the toys.

DEBRA   Oh, Lord, what have I done? Joe was right! Time just gets away from me when I'm on the computer. If I go fast enough and buy some magic erasers, I might get this cleaned up before Joe gets home. Oh, no, I have to get supper ready, so maybe I can just keep him away from the girls' room and clean it up when he goes out. Right, I'll do that.

Debra returns to the kitchen and sees the girls are waiting at the door with shoes on.

DEBRA   Nice, girls, let's go!

SCENE III

INT: KITCHEN-LATE AFTERNOON

Joe is sitting at the kitchen table when Debra comes home with groceries.

DEBRA	Oh my, did the lobsters not show up today?
JOE	Well, that's about as smart as breakfast dishes still in the sink. So girls, tell me, what did Mama feed you for lunch?
SUSAN	Mom made us sandwiches.
DEBRA	Yeah, I was in a rush with laundry and cleaning the house. So, I made something quick so we could get to the grocery store.
JOE	Oh, like the laundry I needed for tonight.
DEBRA	Yes!
JOE	The ones you put in this morning before I left that never made it to the dryer? Am I supposed to wear them wet?

DEBRA	Oh, shoot. I knew I had forgotten to do something before I left.
JOE	So, girls, what kind of sandwich did you have for lunch?
SUSAN	I don't remember.
JOE	Is it because you threw them in the trash?

Debra turns from putting groceries away with a shocked look on her face.

DEBRA	I did not know they did that.
SUSAN	Mama told us to eat fast. I didn't want you to yell again.

Joe looks at Debra and, in a stern voice, says:

JOE	Were you watching them at all today?
DEBRA	I was cleaning up their room while they were supposed to be eating.
JOE	I'll ask you again. Were you watching them at all today? Before you answer, I've been in their room.

Debra rushes around, never looking at Joe, and sends the girls to go play in their room.

DEBRA	I'm sorry I got behind.
JOE	So, no dry clothes, no supper, dishes in the sink, and markers all over the walls and floor.

Joe blocks Debra in a corner, looking her straight in the eye.

JOE	Now, what had you so busy that nothing was getting done as the girls were starving and destroying their room? On the computer again, right?
DEBRA	Well, yes, Tom was having a really bad day and needed someone to talk to.
JOE	Tom, who? Is he a relative, a friend, or an ex-boyfriend?
DEBRA	No, nothing like that. A rule of the chatroom is no last name. I mostly just read what people are saying and how they feel about things. Tom is having problems with his girlfriend, feeling as if she is using him as a babysitter for her son from a past boyfriend. He feels he spent more time babysitting than working on their relationship as a couple.

JOE	You don't belong in another man's problem. This house and the girls are your first priority. If you can't handle that—

The ding goes off on the dryer. Joe starts to walk to the dryer and turns around.

JOE	You know, ever since we got this house, it's been a pig sty.

Joe has his finger pointing right in Debra's face.

(continues)

JOE	You better get your act together around here, or you'll find yourself out the door.

DEBRA	I'm sorry; I'll try to manage my time better.

JOE	I'm going to shower and leave to get me some decent food before meeting up with the guys so they don't learn how lousy of a wife I have.

Joe puts on his jacket and says:

JOE	I'll be home at eleven! This mess and the girls' room best be cleaned up.

Debra cleans up the breakfast dishes. Chicken nuggets and fries for the girls are being cooked.

DEBRA Girls, come for supper! We're going to play magic eraser after in your room, and you girls better never write on the walls or floor again. That makes Daddy really mad.

Debra has them clean for an hour with her and then tells them:

DEBRA I hope you girls know how wrong this was for you to do, and if you ever do it again, you'll be cleaning it all yourself, with no help. Now get in your pjs and go to sleep as Mama finishes your job.

Debra tucks them in bed with a kiss on the forehead as they fall fast asleep. Debra finishes the little that is left and cleans up the area so the room is nice and clean for Joe when he checks it. Not long after that, Debra is back on the computer, and in the chatroom, complaining about Joe. She types these words aggressively.

DEBRA (typing) He's always screaming at me in front of the girls—I mean in my face. I just get so scared and confused when he does that. I can't even think. He just drinks too much, and since he's a lobster man pulling those traps up, I know he's strong. He scares me so much, and the girls are always crying when he's this way.

Debra is talking to herself.

DEBRA   Oh my, thirty-seven people active right now!

Debra starts reading comments from strangers. She says to herself:

DEBRA   Boy, a lot of sympathy and advice. People do understand what I'm going through. Glad there's no last name on here. I better clear my history on here and get to bed before Joe gets home.

Debra shuts down the computer and goes to bed just in time as Joe gets home drunk. He peeks in the bedroom.

JOE   Oh, you're sleeping.

Joe goes on the computer to check out chatrooms.

SCENE IV

INT: KITCHEN-MORNING

Joe is getting his coffee before heading out for another day of fishing.

JOEYou were sleeping when I came home last night, so I thought I'd check out some of those chatrooms that take up so much of your time when I'm out working so hard.

Debra drops a cup of orange juice she was taking to the table for Susan.

(continues)

JOEWhat? You got a problem with that?

DEBRANo. My hand was too wet, and it slipped out.

JOEWell, it seems some people in chatrooms hang out at Mixers. Maybe your Tom goes there?

DEBRAI have no clue. I never asked and only spoke to him that one time.

JOE	Get a sitter for the girls, and we'll go check it out Saturday night.

Debra rushes to half-clean the house to get on the computer. Debra types.

DEBRA	My husband is planning to take me to Mixers on Saturday night, so please, I beg you all not to mention my frustration with him when you see us. I'll be in jeans with a pink sweater and half my hair up. My life is hard enough; please, don't add to it. Thanks

SCENE V

INT: KITCHEN - EARLY EVENING

Debra has supper ready as Joe walks through the door from work. Joe looks at the table and hollers.

JOE		Great! Suppers ready. Time to eat, girls.

Debra nervously pours drinks as Joe takes notice.

JOE		What's your problem today?

DEBRA		I'm not feeling so good today.

JOE		Maybe you need to work harder around here to snap out of it. The place could use a good dusting.

They all get to the table to eat.

JOE		Why are we serving corn as a vegetable with ham? How many times do I have to tell you it's peas with ham? You sure know how to spoil a good meal, don't you? Can't you do anything right? Corn is for chicken; can you get that in your hard head?

DEBRA	Sorry, I bought more corn this week because they were on sale.
JOE	But you can waste money on good steak that you turn into rubber, and we can't eat.
DEBRA	I'm trying to save money for your...
JOE	Go ahead, say it. My beer after a hard day at work?

Debra keeps her head down as she cuts the ham up for the girls.

DEBRA	You're right; I should have bought peas to go with the ham.
JOE	Learn to do things the way I like them, for a change. I'm the one earning the money around here since you're too lazy to work.

Joe continues to eat. The girls are still looking into their plates, not moving at all, till they begin to cry.

DEBRA	Now, Joe, we looked into that before, and I'd only be working to pay for gas and the babysitter. We know how expensive that would be.

Joe gives the girls a sharp glare.

JOE	Girls, eat!

With disdain, Joe looks at his wife again.

JOE	It would at least give you some work experience that I don't see going on around here.
DEBRA	I work plenty around here.
JOE	Oh, yeah! Why do we have a fenced-in yard for the girls, yet I never see them out playing? Too far away from the computer for you to be able to watch them, so they're stuck in their rooms all the time, writing on walls.
DEBRA	The yard needs mowing before the girls go out to play so they aren't in that tall grass.
JOE	So don't be so lazy and mow it.
DEBRA	I don't know how to use a mower. I've never done that before.
JOE	We can take care of that after supper, or do you want one of those old time ones, that you walk and push that don't use gas.

Joe grabs a beer and heads to the living room.

Joe	(continues) Let me know when you're done cleaning the table for your lesson to begin so my girls can have a yard to play in. We don't want to look like we live in a jungle to our neighbors.

The phone rings and Debra runs to answer it as Joe takes notice and goes in the kitchen to listen to what is being said.

DEBRA	Oh, hi, Mom.

Joe talks loud enough for Debra's Mom to hear.

JOE	Mom, you watching the girls Saturday night so we can have a date night?
DEBRA	Mom heard you, and she said, 'Yes.'
JOE	Thanks, Mom. Well, I guess I better put clothes in the washer, so I have something to wear tomorrow. Thanks again, Mom.

Debra is still on the phone with her mother as Joe is around the corner, listening.

DEBRA	I know, Mom. I should stay on top of it all.

Debra rolls her eyes as she turns around, knowing what Joe is doing.

DEBRA	Yes, Mom, see you tomorrow. Bye, love yah!

Debra hangs up, and Joe comes around the corner with a big grin on his face.

DEBRA	Did you get your clothes in the washer?

In a sarcastic voice, Joe says:

JOE	I don't know how to do it. I've never done that before. Now, let's go to the garage and show you how to run a lawn mower.
DEBRA	Let me double-check on the girls and make sure they're in bed with their show on.
JOE	I'll grab a beer and meet you in the garage.

FADE OUT:

SCENE VI

EXT: EARLY EVENING-BACKYARD

FADE IN:

By the time Debra enters the garage, Joe is on his third beer, lining them up.

JOE	So what's the first thing you should do?
DEBRA	Make sure you have gas.
JOE	Well, lucky for you, I labeled the cans so you don't cost me money on repairs. So fill it up.

Debra grabs the correct can and gets ready to fill it up.

JOE	Stop right there, stupid. I don't want gas all over the machine or the floor of the garage, so get the funnel and don't spill any.
DEBRA	Alright, just to make you happy, but I know how to pour.
JOE	So what do you do next, smarty pants?
DEBRA	Start it up and mow.

JOE   Look out there. Can you see where the toys are?

No? So walk your lazy ass around and pick them all up so you don't cost me an arm and a leg on blades.

Debra spends almost an hour to find all the toys as daylight is fading as Joe continues to drink and lining them up.

JOE   Do you see now how much work I was doing after a hard day in the hot sun pulling traps. Now get on there and start the mowing.

Joe shows Debra the gas, brakes, and how to shift.

JOE   (continues) Now mow so the grass cuts and goes to the center of the yard, so no grass goes in the road to cause a motorcycle accident.

DEBRA   Got it.

Debra makes her first pass and goes to do a second.

JOE   Stop! You go like a circle. Look at the grass you just put on the road. Go around always with the grass going inward. Can you understand that?

DEBRA   Yes, dear. I got it now.

Six bottles of beer are now lined up. Joe takes a nap while Debra mows the yard. He wakes up when the mower shuts off.

DEBRA   Looks good, and I got it all done.

JOE   Now put the toys back in the yard and go sweep what you put on the road. I expect to see the girls out playing when I get home from now on.

Debra walks in tired.

DEBRA   I'm going to bed.

Joe goes for another beer and heads to the computer to join chatrooms and writes:

JOE   Hello, everyone! Debra and I will be at Mixers chat night tomorrow. Hope to see you all there.

FADE OUT:

ACT II

SCENE I

INT: MIXERS CHAT DANCE HALL-EVENING

They drop the girls off at Debra's mom. They're all dressed up with their first name only on the tags.

FADE IN:

They see bathrooms in the dance hall when they first walk in. The bar is on the left side of the hall. The walls are sky blue with glowing stars to reflect the disco ball that turns in the center as country music plays. Debra's face lights us as Joe takes notice.

DEBRA	Look, Joe, there's a guy named Tom. I wonder if that is the guy I've talked to once.
JOE	Let's go find out after we get a beer.

They start walking towards Tom.

TOM	So you're Debra, and you must be Joe.
DEBRA	Yes, this is my husband, Joe.
TOM	I've heard a lot about you.
JOE	(sternly) Like what?

TOM	Like you're an ex-marine and now a lobster men. Thank you for your service!
JOE	Oh, yeah. That's right; thanks! Let's dance, my dear.

Debra and Joe dance on the dance floor. As the night moves on, Joe makes sure to make his way around the room as he keeps drinking.

JOE	Why are they all looking at you? Why do all these people look like trash? All chatroom people look like trash.
DEBRA	Joe, not so loud. I met you in a chatroom when you were in the service about to come home, remember?

Joe grabs Debra harshly in haste as all are watching him closely.

JOE	Well, that's different. Computers weren't well known back then. Now, every low-scum trash has one. Why are they looking at us? Let's get out of here.
DEBRA	You're too loud. It's early, and I want to stay longer.

Joe grabs her by the arm tightly and walks towards the Exit. Tom and a few other guys start towards Joe, but they see Debra shaking her head as she is being pulled to the door. They stop and watch her leave.

FADE OUT:

SCENE II

EXT: NEXT MORNING - MOWING LAWN

FADE IN:

JOE   You, get out here and pick these toys up so I can mow the yard. Get out here. NOW!

The neighbors watch as Debra rushes out, quickly picking all the toys around the outside of the fenced-in play yard. Susan and Alley are in the fenced-in play yard when Joe starts yelling. Alley, the three-year-old, runs to her older sister, who is standing still, and grabs her legs.

JOE   (continues) You know, if you got your ass off that computer and cleaned up each day after the girls like you're supposed to, I could get my work done on weekends.

Joe gets off the mower to go after another beer. Picking up the toys Debra missed and throwing them at Debra.

JOE   You missed it. Can you see it now? I'm going to keep mowing, so you better move faster.

DEBRA Stop it! I'm picking them up.

Joe stops and sits there drinking while watching Debra.

JOE   You know I mow on weekends; you should have had this picked up for the weekend. Why do you go out of your way to always make me mad?

DEBRA You can mow the whole front of the house while I finish picking the toys around the fenced area.

JOE   I could have had this all done by now and been relaxing before starting another hard week. Your laziness better change around here.

SCENE III

INT: KITCHEN – NOON

Joe enters the house and grabs a beer and the phone. He presses the redial. An unfamiliar male voice comes on. Joe slams the phone down.

JOE	Who the hell were you talking to?
DEBRA	No one! It was a wrong number.
SUSAN	Mommy, you told them Daddy was mad and you would tell them tomorrow.

Joe walks up to Debra and pushes her up against the wall.

JOE	What shit are you trying to pull on me now?
DEBRA	Nothing; they just wondered why we left so early last night. I told them it just wasn't our type of place.

Joe gives another hard push, spitting his words in Debra's face.

DEBRA	Stop it! You're hurting my back.
JOE	You better not be lying to me if you know what's good for you. You're the

one driving me to drink. I can't trust you or believe in you anymore. Even the girls know better and point out your lies. See what you're teaching them!

Joe grabs another beer and goes to watch television. Debra gets the girls to bed and goes to bed herself with a hurting back.

SCENE IV

INT: EARLY MORNING

Joe grabs his lunch and starts toward the door. Before Joe leaves, Debra puts in her thoughts.

DEBRA Joe, dear, I wish you would stop grabbing a drink after work. It's not good for the girls to see us fighting so much. You have picked up drinking so much in the past month, and it's causing us problems.

Joe twists Debra around, so she is now facing him.

JOE It's your fault I'm drinking so much. You're always trying to pull something over on me. If you weren't so lazy and did things around here to help out or pull your weight, I wouldn't have to drink at all.

Debra tries to break loose from Joe's grip.

JOE (continues) Don't you dare blame me. Get your act together and things will straighten up around here.

Joe goes out the door for work, slamming the door behind him. Debra washes the breakfast dishes and takes the Hamburg out to make chop suey for supper with garlic bread. She then takes out the trash and puts a load of Joe's fishing clothes in the washer. She sees the computer and can't help but want to release the painful frustration of the weekend out.

DEBRA (writes on computer) This weekend was hell. The more Joe drank, the worse it got for me. Joe slammed me against the wall so hard twice that my back is all black and blue today.

Debra notices more people are signed in the group than before, but they do not give her the support she had been getting previously.

DEBRA You girls may go play in the play yard, but no throwing toys over the fence. You know that makes Daddy really mad.

Debra is heading to the dryer as the phone rings.

DEBRA Hi, Tom. You really mustn't call when Joe is home. He is very mad and suspects I'm doing whatever stuff behind his back that he has created in his head. Tell the gang I need things to

	cool down and not give him any reason to doubt me so he can cool his drinking and anger.

All is quiet for a moment as Tom processes her words.

DEBRA	Yeah, I have a black and blue imprint on my arm from him grabbing me Saturday night, but that's little compared to the bruises he left on my back on Sunday. It's been one hell of a weekend.

Another moment of silence as Debra starts cooking supper.

DEBRA	I'm used to it. Be cool; it'll be alright. Maybe I do need to do more around here, as he has said so many times. I need to make life easier around here for him. I've got to get supper ready before he gets home. Please tell everyone to stay cool, and I'll see you all on Wednesday night at Bingo.

Debra had supper ready on the table, with the girls seated, when Joe came walking through the door from work.

JOE	This is what I should come home to every night after a long, hard day at work.

DEBRA	I made plans with my sister, Doris, for Wednesday night Bingo.
JOE	Yeah, It's your week to go out. I'm going out with a few of the dock people from work tonight after supper.
DEBRA	Why? You went out twice last week.
JOE	I'll go out every night if I want to. I make the money around here; don't you forget it. Get my blue pants and matching shirt ready for me after my shower, or do you want me to go out Wednesday night, too?
DEBRA	Yes, dear.

As Joe and the girls are eating, Debra pulls clothes from the dryer for Joe and sets them in the bathroom rack before joining them for supper.

DEBRA	Okay, girls, go play in your rooms while Daddy takes a shower and Mom cleans up the table.

When Joe gets out of the shower, he gets right up in Debra's face as she is washing dishes. Holding one white sock and one black sock.

JOE	What the hell is this white sock doing with one black sock? You gone blind now, or just want to piss me off? What did you do with the other black sock? Want me going out looking like a clown?

Debra is frozen in place, not daring to move.

JOE	Where the hell's my other black sock?
DEBRA	I'm sorry; I'll go find it right away. It must have fallen between the washer and dryer when I went to answer the phone. I didn't notice it.
JOE	Who the hell's calling you?
DEBRA	My mother called when I was putting the clothes in the dryer. I went to clean up in the girls' room after that and hadn't noticed dropping one. I'll get you another pair from your drawer.

Joe turns and walks away as he mutters.

JOE	You better smarten up, girl. I mean it!

Debra shows a sign of relief as Joe walks out the door for a night out with the guys from the dock.

SCENE V

INT: NEXT DAY – EARLY EVENING

Debra is excited to get out of the house to go play Bingo, which is something she likes and does well at.

JOE	You make sure you call at half-time and come home before ten.
DEBRA	I'll surely be right home when Bingo is done.
JOE	Who are you going to meet there?
DEBRA	My sister. Doris; no one else. You know the hall is full of people. Bye, dear.

As Debra leaves, Joe sends the girls to their room and goes on the computer. He figures out Debra's password. He knows to only read the mail Debra has already read. He goes to the fridge to grab a beer and then continues to read her mail. He reads a particular one out loud from Tom.

Tom	Debra, you should take the girls and leave him.

Joe gets mad and puts his fist through the wall. The girls come running.

Susan	Daddy, what happened?
JOE	Daddy just turned too fast and hit the wall. Let's go to bed now, girls.

FADE OUT:

SCENE VI

INT: EVENING BINGO HALL – EVENING

FADE IN:

CAROL   So, Debra, tell us about last weekend.

DEBRA   Well, it's mostly what I said in the chatroom. Joe pushed me hard against the wall twice. I mean hard; he's not only strong from pulling lobster traps all day, but he's also a Marine.

CAROL   That must have hurt!

KEVIN   You said you have bruises?

DEBRA   My shoulders are sore, and look at this!

Debra shows the group both sides of her shoulders, then the grab marks of Saturday night.

DEBRA   (continues) That's nothing compared to the rest of my body. My back got the worst of it.

KEVIN   No man should ever treat a woman like that.

The rest of the group (mostly men) stares at Debra in shock.

JOHNATHAN   You know, Debra, there are good women groups who can put you and the girls in a safe house while you get divorced to keep him away.

DEBRA   If I did that, he'd find me, and my life would be over.

JOHNATHAN   Well, give it some serious thought and know we're all here for you.

DEBRA   Thanks, guys; chatting and getting it all out is helping me live with strength day by day.

FADE OUT:

INT: EVENING – HOME

The phone rings.

JOE   That must be Mom. Now, girls, go to bed now!

HELLO!

DEBRA   It's half-time. So far, I won fifty dollars. It was a hundred-dollar game, but I had to split it with another player.

JOE   Who's there?

DEBRA   Well, I got to go get ready; another game is about to start. Bye…

Joe returns to the computer and pretends to be Debra in the chatroom. He discovers they had been talking about his cruelty and unfairness. He reads all the exchanged texts.

JACKIE   Even my husband, Sam, says your Joe is nothing but danger for you. It's clear abuse and controlling what he's done. Get yourself out of there and protect those poor little girls from him. That's your job as a mom.

It's 10:30, and Debra is just driving in. Joe goes for another beer as Debra walks in.

JOE	You're late! Where did you go after bingo?
DEBRA	Nowhere; winner-takes-all was long.
JOE	Yeah, right! I told you to be home by ten. I know bingo doesn't last that long.

Joe gets in Debra's face like he is going to bite her nose off. Debra turns, heading toward the bedroom. Joe steps in front of her.

JOE	Where did you go?
DEBRA	I told you nowhere.
JOE	Oh! Did the gang all stay to talk about how mean and cruel I am? Is that what took you so damn long?
DEBRA	Joe, you've had too much to drink. Don't wake the girls up. Let's go to bed.
JOE	Yeah, right, bitch. Face it, you're lying to me again. Are you sleeping around on me? Huh? Tell me! Tell me now! Tell it to my face now, huh? Huh!

DEBRA   Let's go to bed, Joe. You're drunk.

Joe pushes Debra out of his path, and she hits the corner of the counter and begins to bleed.

DEBRA   Joe, I'm bleeding.

Joe storms to the bedroom without paying her attention. Debra finds a big band-aid and cleans up the blood as she hears Joe yelling.

JOE   Come to me, you lying, cheating, lazy baby.

Debra waits till she hears Joe snoring before softly getting into bed.

SCENE VII

INT: NEXT DAY – MID-MORNING

Debra gets on the computer to talk about what happened after bingo.

PAUL	Debra, how can you be at bingo when you were on here, chatting with us last night?
TOM	No, Paul; she was with us at bingo.
DEBRA	Oh, no, that means Joe was on here pretending to be me. I must have forgotten to clear my history.
KEVIN	Time for you to get out of there with the girls.
DEBRA	I have to go and get groceries done. I need to think about this.

FADE OUT:

INT: AFTERNOON

Joe gets home early from work and looks around for a note.

JOE	God damn her. Where the hell is the fucking note. Where the hell is she now?

Joe grabs a beer and sits at the window overlooking the driveway. He thinks about what was said on the computer. He grabs another beer as he looks for something to eat. He slams the fridge door and sits down as Debra drives in.

Joe	Where's my note?
DEBRA	Sorry, I was running late and didn't expect you to be home so early.
JOE	Who were you with all this time? I've been home for an hour.
DEBRA	No one, Joe, just the girls. I went to do groceries after the girls woke up from their nap. My back is sore, so I'm moving slower so it can heal.
JOE	Oh, hell, you wouldn't know the truth if it got up and bit you on the nose. You fix me something to eat while I go shower.

DEBRA Yes, dear.

Debra can only think of hamburgers in that short time between running to the car and getting groceries. Joe is out of the shower and dressed for the night out with the boys.

JOE How much did you steal from me this time for this hamburger supper?

DEBRA I only spent what I won at bingo.

JOE So, you lied about that, too?

DEBRA No, I won fifty before half-time and 100.00 on letter X during the blackout, which is the long last game of the night.

Joe leaves to go out with the guys. Debra knows to clean the house and be in bed before Joe gets home drunk again.

SCENE VIII

INT: BEDROOM – MIDNIGHT

Joe returns home and walks into the bedroom tipsy to Debra's side of the bed, pushing her awake.

JOE	I want to know the truth now. Who are you sleeping with now? Is it Tom? Steve? Which one of those assholes is it?

DEBRA	Joe, I've talked to them in chat rooms only. I'm not sleeping with anyone. Now get in bed and get some sleep.

Joe grabs Debra by the throat, and she starts gasping for air like a fish out of water.

JOE	You're a lying bitch. I ought to kill you right now.

Debra manages to kick him in the groin and runs to phone the police. This makes the wound on her back reopen, and blood starts dripping down on the floor.

DEBRA	Help me! Help me!

Joe pulls the phone out of the wall. As he crushes it with his feet, Susan comes running out of her bedroom.

SUSAN	Mommy, what's happening? Why is Daddy mad?
DEBRA	Susan, take your sister and run out to the car. Fast!

Susan picks up Alley and runs out of the house, crying loudly. She starts running down the dark streets in fear. Debra tries to grab the car keys.

JOE	Where do you think you're going, bitch? That's my car; I paid for it.

Joe grabs Debra again by the throat.

DEBRA	Joe, you're choking me!
JOE	Shut up, bitch, or I'll plug your nose up, too.

Debra screams as she pushes Joe and tries to make her way out the door. Joe grabs her by the arm, flipping her on her bruised back, reopening her wound from the previous night even more.

EXT: YARD – MIDNIGHT

DEBRA　　　　　Stop, you'll kill me. Think of the girls!

JOE　　　　　　You want me to? I can do it. I was trained to be really good! I need another beer.

Joe goes into the house to grab another beer as Debra, who is bleeding hard, gets in the car to get away.

In the meantime, the police were able to trace the call and were on their way to Debra's house. The cop spots two little girls crying loudly while trying to run in the dark of the night. Susan is just in her underpants, and Alley is in a diaper. The officer stops and calls for backup to go to the residence.

OFF. HARPER　　Hello, I'm Officer Harper. What's your name?

SUSAN　　　　　I'm Susan (cries), and this is my sister, Alley. Daddy is mad, and Mama told me to get Alley and get in the car. Oh no, I didn't do that.

Susan turns around with Alley to go back to the car.

OFF. HARPER   Susan, you and Alley, come with me to the station, and we will get Mom so you're all safe. Okay?!

The girls get in the cruiser, and the officer sees blood on Susan's feet.

OFF. HARPER   Susan, did you get hurt? (pointing to Susan's feet)

SUSAN   No, that's Mom's blood.

Officer Harper arrives at the station.

OFF. HARPER   Advice those being dispatched to that address, we may be looking at a DOA. Mother's blood on one of the girls. Clothes will also be needed for the girls.

OFF. HARPER   Susan, how old are you and your sister?

SUSAN   I'm 5, and Alley is 3.

DISPATCHER   We hear that and will make the arrangements for the night and take it from there.

The officer walks Susan and Alley into the station. One of the dispatchers takes the girls to the bathroom to clean them up and get clothes on them.

DISP. ELLAN   Would you, girls, like some chocolate milk and cookies?

SUSAN   Yes, we would.

Alley is scared and holding on to Susan tightly as Ellan gives them a snack and puts a children's show on for them to watch and relax.

ACT III

SCENE I

EXT: ON THE ROAD – 3:00 A.M.

The police find Debra driving on the road, looking for Susan and Alley. They stop her.

OFF. GORDON   Are you Debra?

DEBRA   Yes, Officer, yes. Do you have my girls? Where are they?

OFF. GORDON   I'm Officer Gordon. Your girls are safe.

DEBRA   I got to go get them. Where are they?

OFF. GORDON   You don't want to traumatize them any more than they already are by having them see you like this. I'm calling you an ambulance. Dispatch, get me an ambulance at 79 Bates Street.

DEBRA   I don't need an ambulance. I need my girls.

OFF. GORDON   We can let you have your girls when the hospital checks you out and give us the okay. Here's a blanket. I see a lot of blood all over your clothes, and your neck will need an X-ray for sure.

The ambulance arrives. They first start by putting a neck brace on Debra, then load her up in the ambulance.

OFF. GORDON   Don't worry about the girls. They will remain in our care till you're able to care for them again.

INT: HOSPITAL EMERGENCY ROOM

Debra arrives unconscious.

DR. JONES Let's get her to the OR and get her airway opened up. Get her blood type and blood over to the OR for her.

Next, Debra is being rushed to the OR.

DR. JONES We'll save her. Stay sideline so our staff can move clearly.

OFF. GORDON Dispatch, she is in the OR right now, getting her throat opened up so she can breathe on her own. They also called for blood. She will be here a few days if all goes well. Place the girls in a safe home for their protection, as we will be adding attempted murder charges on her husband. The location of the girls is not to be known to anyone out there.

DISPATCHER Copy that! We'll assign a guard for her at all times.

Dr. Jones comes out of the OR two hours later.

DR. JONES We saved her, but she will be placed in critical care for her back issues. We'll

	be sending her to an X-ray to see if we're dealing with internal bleeding as well. She lost a lot of blood and also has old wounds, so we don't know if it's all from this incident or others in recent days. X-rays will give us a better idea, and I will let you know when she will be well enough to question.
OFF. GORDON	I understand.
DR. JONES	Have the next of kin been contacted?
OFF. GORDON	Not yet! We've been busy with her husband's arrest and placing two little girls in a safe home.
DR. JONES	Have the staff get a hold of me so I can talk to them before they see her.
OFF. GORDON	Will do doc.

The doctor walks away.

FADE OUT:

SCENE II

INT: 4:00 A.M. AT THE HOME

In the meantime, officers head to the house to make the arrest of Debra's husband, Joe. The officers arrive at the house and can clearly see a fight has taken place. The phone is smashed on the floor. Coats that must have been hanging are now on the floor and all over the place. They spot a lot of blood outside, as well as some on the floor, showing the path Debra had taken. There are holes punched out in the wall. Joe is passed out on the couch.

FADE IN:

Joe is woken by the police.

OFF. BLISS Joe, we are arresting you for spousal abuse, failure to allow your wife to call us, having been drunk and disorderly, and for attempted murder.

JOE I'll be out by morning; you watch. The bitch will drop the charges, and I'll get my girls.

Joe is read his rights and taken to jail.

FADE OUT:

Joe gets his one phone call.

JOE Mom, I need you to bail me out. Debra got charges put on me last night for arguing with her.

MRS. LISA CROW (Joe's mother) Were you drinking?

JOE Yeah, I had a few.

MRS. LISA CROW Son, you know you can't drink on the medicine the VA has you on.

JOE   Well, come to court at 10:00 and bail me out so I can go to work and get you the money back.

MRS. LISA CROW   You should have had them take you to the VA so you could be protected from all of this.

JOE   Yeah, and they would have kept me all through lobster season. Now, how can I pay the bills like that?

MRS. LISA CROW   I'll get you a criminal lawyer and explain your PTSD condition ever since you returned from Iraq. Maybe that can help you get out of this with just some consoling.

JOE   Okay, Ma, so you'll bail me out?

MRS. LISA CROW   Yes, dear.

SCENE III

INT: COURT

Before the bail hearing, the lawyer talks to Joe's mother.

MR. BATES　　Mrs. Bates, are you aware of the charges being brought against your son in this court?

MRS. LISA CROW　　Joe said they had an argument, and Debra got him arrested.

MR. BATES　　Joe is charged with spousal abuse, failure to allow Debra to call the police, being drunk and disorderly, and attempted murder. Debra went through surgery and is in critical condition in the hospital right now. Do you really want him to live in your home until the court proceedings are over?

With a tear running down her face, she answers.

MRS. LISA CROW　　He's my wounded military son. It's not his fault he came home this way. I wish they knew how to better help them adjust to life when they come home this way. Yes, I'll take him in. I have to!

The judge walks into the courtroom. The court is in order.

MR. BATES Your Honor, what we have here is a veteran who was not aware of how his actions would be if he had a drink out with the guys while taking his medication. We're willing to take bail till his court date, as this is his first offense with VA consoling.

JUDGE CORNAIL I can see there is no prior, but these are very serious charges. Do you understand the seriousness of what you have been charged with?

JOE Yes, Sir, I do.

JUDGE CORNAIL Do you have someone to stay with till your court hearing is done, and are they present here in court today?

JOE Yes, Sir, my mother's here.

JUDGE CORNAIL Will the mother please stand?

Mrs. Lisa Crow stands up.

JUDGE CORNAIL Do you understand the seriousness of these charges, and are

	you willing to take him into your home till these court proceedings are complete?
MRS. LISA CROW	Yes, I do, and I will.
JUDGE CORNAIL	Will you have all alcohol removed from your home and not allow any in till these court proceedings are done, knowing you may be charged if you allow alcohol in any form in your home?
MRS. LISA CROW	Yes, Sir, I understand.
JUDGE CORNAIL	I order you to seek professional help within 3 days and provide that proof to the courts. You're to reside at your mother's only, and you will be visited to make sure you are there. No alcohol at any time. An ankle bracelet that will allow you to go to work and back will be issued. You are not in any way, shape, or form to contact your wife or the children till this court allows you to. No direct or indirect contact at all. Do you understand what I have just said to you?
JOE	Yes, Sir.

JUDGE CORNAIL   I also set your fine at $3,000.00.

The judge leaves the courtroom. Joe turns to his mother.

JOE   Mom, do you have that much money?

MRS. LISA CROW   Only if you pay it back in the next few weeks. I still have my monthly payments to make. You didn't tell me about the attempted murder charges.

JOE   Just made up stuff to make me look worse than I was, Mom.

MR. BATES   Joe, you're all bailed out, so stay away from Debra and the girls. Get some help from the VA and let me know who it is in three days so I can file it with the courts, or they'll issue an arrest warrant, and you'll have to stay in jail till court, and that's two months away. No drinking or getting in any trouble with the law. Just go to work and back to your Mom's. Got it!

JOE   Yeah, I got it. The bitch has me over a barrel.

MRS. LISA CROW   That's enough of that, Joe. Now, let's go.

FADE OUT:

INT: HOME

Mrs. Lisa Crow takes Joe home to where his brother Tim, who is his partner, also lives.

FADE IN:

TIM	Thank God you're out. Now, tomorrow will be a double workload.
JOE	Hopefully, we can make Mom her $3,000.00 she used to bail me out.
TIM	Don't take that from my share. Your mess is not mine.
JOE	Can't you help a brother out?!
TIM	I still have a life to live, and I need to go out with girls.
JOE	What have you been doing with the money you've been making since you get everything for free as Mom's golden boy?
TIM	The house next door is about to come up for sale. I'll be getting it.
JOE	I always get the raw deals.

MRS. LISA CROW   Joe, have you called the VA to get a consular yet?

JOE   Not yet. Give me a break.

MRS. LISA CROW   The court needs a person in three days, and you know the VA dosen't move that fast. No time to waste.

JOE   Tim, don't get yourself a woman. They'll drive you to drink from nagging you to death.

MRS. LISA CROW   Joe, you don't sit twitting your thumb when you have attempted murder charges hanging over your head.

TIM   What? So you're the person everyone is talking about who got an ambulance called for choking a woman!

JOE   No ambulance came to the house. That must have been someone else.

TIM   They found her driving all bloody and with marks on her throat, looking for her children.

JOE   Where did you hear that?

TIM	On the news. She went through surgery and is in intensive care with a police guard at her door.
JOE	What happened to the kids?
TIM	They're not saying, so they must be in a safe home with you having attempted murder charges.
JOE	They should have called one of you to take them.
MRS. LISA CROW	They would have called Debra's family to take them, not us at all.
JOE	That bitch wins again.
MRS. LISA CROW	Joe, will you listen to yourself? Your wife just had surgery and is in critical condition and may die. You can be looking at life in jail.
JOE	You don't understand. She was unfaithful to me and talking trash about me in chat rooms on the computer.
MRS. LISA CROW	First of all, Joe, I don't believe she was unfaithful. She may not have been Marine Corp organized, but she had to love you to have put up with what you

have been dishing out. Still, it's no reason to almost kill the mother of your children.

Joe changes the subject.

JOE I'm hungry. What's for supper?

Tim gets up and goes to the kitchen to get a drink while his mother tells Joe the home rules.

MRS. LISA CROW Joe, the house rules for you are the same as those for your brother. Free rent, but care for yourself. I'm not your girlfriend or your wife. Fix meals for yourself so they're fixed just how you like them. At my age, I have enough taking care of myself and cleaning up any messes you make. Understood?

JOE See, Tim, that's a woman's attitude.

MRS. LISA CROW Right! Learn from it.

Joe goes into the kitchen to fix himself a sandwich. Tim whispers to his mother.

TIM What on earth have you brought into your house?

Tim's Mom shrugs her shoulders as if to say, 'I don't know.' Joe walks back into the room with a sandwich and soda.

JOE	Ma, you should call to find out where the girls are. If Debra is in the hospital, as their father, I have a right, and I want my girls with me.
MRS. LISA CROW	No, Joe. I'm not putting myself in the middle of this.
JOE	Listen here, old lady; they're my girls. You have the room, and I want them with me.
TIM	Oh, Joe.
MRS. LISA CROW	You best watch how you talk to me, son. You need to work to pay your bills, and I'm too old to be a babysitter, grandchild or not. These are little, active girls. The courts said to stay away from them. No direct or indirect contact. Did you already forget that? You want to be in jail now?
JOE	Oh, I forgot that part, but you know, if I was your golden child, you'd do it anyway.

MRS. LISA CROW	I did what I could, and if you're not grateful for that, then I'm sorry for you.
TIM	Don't look at me. I'm not getting in the middle of this.
JOE	No balls, huh?
TIM	Now, we have two days of lobsters in our traps. What time we heading out in the morning?
JOE	Day break, say 5:00 A.M. So we're on the water by six.
TIM	I did pick up bait today. Didn't know what else to do.
JOE	Good, one less thing to do in the morning.
TIM	Okay, I got to head out, and I'll be home by eight for an early start tomorrow. Joe, do yourself a favor bro and get some sleep. You look tired and stressed out. Will talk tomorrow, okay?

With this, Tim walks out of the house.

FADE OUT:

SCENE IV

INT. EARLY MORNING – HOSPITAL

FADE IN:

In the hospital, a social worker pays Debra a visit.

MISS. JENNA DAVIS   Hello, Debra, they told us you were awake. I'm Miss Jenna Davis. I want you to know your girls are safe and in an undisclosed home for their protection. They're fine physically but are having nightmares at night. This is normal to see after what we believe they have been through.

Debra tries to talk but can't, and the worker rings the bell for a nurse. Nurses come running.

MISS JENNA DAVIS   She tried to talk but couldn't.

One nurse gives her water, and the other nurse brings her a whiteboard to write what she wants to say.

DEBRA   *(writes)* He will find them!

MISS JENNA DAVIS   No, Debra, they are at a secret location, and we were very careful keeping it that way, even from you or any family member without court papers. In this case, we don't see that happening.

DEBRA   *(writes)* Where is Joe right now? Jail?

MISS JENNA DAVIS   No, Ma'am, he's out on bail, living at his mother's. She bailed him out.

DEBRA   *(writes)* Police need to protect her.

MISS JENNA DAVIS   Joe has an ankle bracelet that allows him to go to work and back to his mother's only. He can't go drinking, and no alcohol is allowed in the home. So you don't have to worry. They are also patrolling her street every hour he is there. Did you know your husband has PTSD?

DEBRA   *(writes)* Yes, I tried to get him help. He went once and said the guy was a kook and didn't even know enough to get a haircut or shave.

MISS JENNA DAVIS   Well, he has three days to get into counseling as part of his bail condition. He was mixing his VA medicine with all that alcohol he was drinking. Enough to prove insanity if he wants to, and I expect his lawyer will.

DEBRA *(writes)* When do I get out of here?

MISS JENNA DAVIS It will be a few more days before they recheck your throat, as you need to be well enough to talk. They will also have to wait for you to be able to eat solid food without causing the throat to become irritated again or swell up. You also lost a lot of blood, so you need to relax and gain your strength back. Don't worry about the girls. They have children their age to play with and are being watched at all times with someone to talk their feelings out, too.

DEBRA *(writes)* Thank you so very much.

MISS JENNA DAVIS I'll come back in a few days to give you updates on the girls and how they're doing.

FADE OUT:

SCENE V

EXT: EARLY MORNING.- DOWN AT THE DOCK

Joe and Tim are at the fisherman's dock, walking to Joe's lobster boat, which was passed onto him by a family member. As he unlatches the rope, Joe notices people he's never seen before in the area. His brother, Tim, notices the same.

FADE IN:

JOE	Hey Tim! Have you noticed all the new people around here all of a sudden?
TIM	Yeah, and they don't look like they're doing much either.
JOE	We must be about to hit peak season early this year.
TIM	Well, maybe that's why they're watching us. Probably don't understand why we haven't hired an extra crew yet.

JOE	Oh, well, more money for us. Looks like I'm gonna need it. I've already run up a bill for a criminal lawyer, and he tells me I'm going to waste around a thousand in AA classes, along with other trash shit, just to keep my ass out of jail. Not to mention his price for the trail.

Tim looks at the people that seem to be surrounding them.

TIM	What are you guys looking at? Get out of here; we're not hiring.
JOE	Let's head out, Tim, and check our traps.

They race out to the open waters and only slow down when they reach their traps.

TIM	You know, Joe, at the dock, I was getting the feeling we were being watched—way too early in the morning for so many job seekers.
JOE	I have felt that way ever since Mom bailed me out of jail. Every time I turn around, there seems to be someone watching me, but I don't recognize

	any of them. It seems to be different people all the time.
TIM	Well, there's a lot of people looking for jobs these days. They must know you're a fisherman by the way you look.
JOE	Yeah, I must have that walk or smell, right?

They both laugh out loud.

TIM	We're full, and our fuel is getting low.
JOE	Okay, we'll have to start from here tomorrow till we get caught up for a day lost.
TIM	I'll bring extra fuel so we don't get this low tomorrow.
JOE	Okay, we'll be out here late today by the time we get this all unloaded.
TIM	Maybe we can get a few of those dock people to help us just for the day and pay cash?
JOE	If I wasn't so tired, I'd say no cause I need the cash, but for today, alright.

They get to the dock, and no extra workers are in sight.

TIM   Oh, great.

JOE   Look at the time. They got tired or gave up and went home. Grab an energy drink, and let's get this unloaded.

FADE OUT:

INT: EVENING – JOE'S MOM'S HOUSE

Joe and Tim finally get to their mom's house.

MRS. LISA CROW   How was your day, boys?

She doesn't give them time to answer.

MRS. LISA CROW   Well, mine was just nerve-racking. This is a dead-end road, and cars have been driving back and forth all day.

TIM   I didn't see no yard sale signs, and the only house that will be coming up for sale is next door, and they promised to let me know when that time comes.

JOE   Mom, we had the same problem this morning at the dock, but by the time we got our catch and back at the dock, no one was in sight.

MRS. LISA CROW   Joe, I don't like this. If it doesn't go away, you'll have to find another place to live.

JOE   Ma, they probably heard about what happened in the paper and are curious. It will blow over like everything else in life does.

MRS. LISA CROW   It better, Joe. I'm too old for this.

TIM	Let me shower up, then I'll go get us some warm food before we hit the bed for another heavy day.

JOE	We got to start at the end and move forward with 3 days of lobster in those traps.

FADE OUT:

SCENE VI

INT: MORNING AT THE HOSPITAL

Miss Jenna Davis, the social worker, visits Debra again.

FADE IN:

MISS JENNA DAVIS Debra, I have a few visitors for you. The girls come running in.

Tears of joy come running down Debra's face.

DEBRA Oh, my darlings, how are you? I missed you two so much.

MISS JENNA DAVIS We're here to take you home this morning. The nurse will be in shortly with your discharge papers. An officer is at your home checking everything out, as is your mom. I'll spend the afternoon with you setting things back up and going on small errands, like getting your medications if need be.

SUSAN Mom, we stayed at a real policeman's house, and he had girls for us to play with. It was like going on a vacation.

ALLEY	I want their play yard, Mommy.
DEBRA	Well, dear, give Mommy time to get back on her feet, and we'll see what we can do. Okay?

FADE OUT:

INT: EARLY AFTERNOON – DEBRA'S HOUSE

They reach Debra's house and are greeted by Officer Bliss.

OFFICER BLISS	Welcome home, Debra. Your home is secured.
SUSAN	Mommy, he's the policeman who was taking care of us.
DEBRA	Well, you guys in blue have surely gone beyond the call of duty. I appreciate you, and thank you so much for caring for my precious girls.
OFF. BLISS	Look, Alley, what I added to your play yard.
ALLEY	Can I go play, Mom? Please?
DEBRA	Sure you can, dear.
ALLEY	Thank you, policeman, you're the best. Come, Sis.
OFF. BLISS	She spent most of her time on the trampoline, and if it helps her, then so be it.
MISS JENNA DAVIS	Thank you, officer. Debra, while the girls play, we should clean out the mess in the house so they don't have to see it. I see your mom

already cleaned the blood outside here.

Debra starts walking into the house and turns on the top of the stairs to say:

DEBRA	Thank you again, Officer Bliss.

MISS JENNA DAVIS	I see your mom's been busy cleaning up so the girls don't have to see anything.

BARBARA	*(Debra's mom)* Hello, Miss Davis. I'm Barbara, Debra's Mom. They let me in yesterday to get the house back in order and cleaned up. I just got back with groceries and was just putting them away. They said they would be patrolling the area, so we do not have to worry if we see them driving by all night.

MISS JENNA DAVIS	I see everything is in order, so I'll leave you two be. Don't hesitate to call if you need any help, Debra.

DEBRA	Thank you for bringing me home and giving me updates on my girls. I appreciate it all. Thanks!

The girls come in for something to drink.

SUSAN   When is Daddy coming home, Mommy?

DEBRA   Daddy is getting help so he doesn't get mad anymore. So we have to wait and see.

ALLEY   Mama, he scares me.

DEBRA   I know, dear. How about you girls play a little longer outside, then I'll fix you supper. You'll get a bubble bath after supper, okay?

BARBARA   You know, Debra, the officer had a talk with me before you got home and said many women take their husbands back after the ordeal. He said that they get upset when we take their children away from them. He made it clear that if you take Joe back, that will be between you guys. Police will not interfere.

DEBRA   Ma, that would never happen. I know Joe better than anyone, and I will not put my life in his hands again. My girls need their mother now and always.

Debra's looking for a fast supper.

BARBARA   I already fixed Mac & cheese with hot dogs and peas.

DEBRA   Great, Ma. I'm getting tired, and that's a saver for me. Girls, come for supper.

SUSAN   Mommy, where's your car?

DEBRA   Oh, I'll have to put that on my list for first thing to do in the morning.

ALLEY   Are we staying home now?

DEBRA   Yes, dear, now finish eating while Grandma gets your bubble bath going.

BARBARA   Girls, let go choose your pjs and let Mom get some rest.

Barbara speaks to Debra now.

BARBARA   I'll be staying here the night so you can go to bed. I'll handle the girls and get them in bed.

INT: EARLY MORNING

It's six in the morning, and the girls and Debra's Mom are still sleeping. Debra calls Tom.

DEBRA	Tom, it's me, Debra.
TOM	We heard what happened to you. How are you?
DEBRA	My neck is so soar. It's hard to swallow. My back was bleeding so bad that they had to give me blood. So, I'm still weak, but I'm getting better.

Susan starts screaming. Debra drops the phone and goes to her room. She cuddles Susan in her arms.

SUSAN	Mommy, Mommy, is Daddy still mad?
DEBRA	Susan, it's alright. Daddy isn't here. The police took Daddy so he could get some help.

Alley wakes up and goes to Susan's bed so she can cuddle, too.

SUSAN	Mommy, I had a dream that Daddy was hurting you again. My legs are tired, Mommy.

DEBRA	Honey, you just rest, and Mommy will make you a special breakfast, and we'll eat in bed today. Okay? I'll put the T.V. on for you while I go cook something special.

Debra grabs the phone that she had left hanging outside.

DEBRA	Oh, Tom, I'm sorry.
TOM	I heard what your daughter said; I want you to know all your friends in the chatroom are with you. We'll keep an eye on you so he never hurts you or the girls again.
DEBRA	Oh, Tom, I don't know what I'm going to do. I'm so scared. You know he was Marine, and I thought I was a goner for sure that night.
TOM	So, you said he was a fisherman, right?
DEBRA	Yes, he is out on the Portland landing.
TOM	Does he have his own boat?
DEBRA	Yes, but his brother helps him when he's not hung over in the morning, which is a day or two a week.
TOM	You go take care of those girls and fix them a nice, yummy breakfast. I'll go

	to the chatroom and inform the gang. We'll take care of you and stop by to visit. I'll make sure they all know to call first so you don't get scared if you see someone pull in. Okay?
DEBRA	I wonder what happened to my car?
TOM	Let me check on that for you. Take care. Bye!
DEBRA	Bye, and thanks for the help.

The girls are in bed, eating with Mom and Grandma, when they hear a knock at the door. Debra goes to the kitchen, peeking from the curtains, and she sees a police officer.

OFF. HARPER	Debra, I'm here to tell you your car will be delivered any minute now.
DEBRA	Oh, good! I wondered what happened to it.
OFFI. HARPER	We had it impounded, and the charges have been paid, as well as delivery. Oh, here it comes.
DEBRA	Is it safe for me to go to the store here in town? I believe Joe is fishing right now.

OFF. HARPER Yes, Ma'am, we'll be patrolling the area.

FADE OUT:

SCENE VII

EXT: DOWN ON THE DOCK – EARLY MORNING

A new group of people watches Joe and Tim, but they try not to be seen.

JOE	You see that? Did you get the extra fuel?
TIM	Yes, I did, and it's already loaded. I came to help you get the bait loaded, but I got to hit the dentist early this morning, so you'll have to do without me for a few hours. Express care opens at seven, and I know you're going to the end of our traps and working forward. I'll find you after they put a new filling or yank it out.
JOE	Okay, Tim, see me off, and I'll watch you leave. Then, I'll see you in a few hours.
TIM	Look at them acting like sneaks, thinking we don't see them. Let's get

you on the water. We know they'll be gone after.

Tim returns from the dentist and finds where Joe is at. Joe spots Tim and yells out to him.

JOE   We're in the money again today!

Tim begins to unload his small aluminum boat to get out to Joe. He hears the lobster boat engine sound differently and turns in time to see the boat explode. It sounds like it exploded twice. All he could see is black smoke. Lobster pieces fly all the way to shore, where Tim is standing in shock, then he falls back. When he's able to stand back up, he yells.

TIM   JOE, JOE, where are you? What the hell happened?

Tim sees the coast guard arrive at the scene and yells out!

TIM   That's my brother. Find him!

A coast guard boat arrives as Tim is about to enter the water to join Joe in fishing their traps out.

CHARLIE   *(the coast guard)* Sir, what is your name?

TIM   Tim Crow. That was my brother's boat. We fish together.

CHARLIE	What is your brother's name?
TIM	Joe Crow!
CHARLIE	Sir, I'm sorry to inform you your brother died in the explosion.
TIM	Who did this? We've been getting watched for a few days now after Joe's arrest.
CHARLIE	By whom?
TIM	Strangers on the dock, and when we return with our catch, no one is in sight.
CHARLIE	Any known problems with the boat?
TIM	No. Oh my God, if I hadn't gone to the dentist this morning, that would have been me, too. How am I going to tell Mom? She said people were driving by all day yesterday, and we live on a dead-end street.
CHARLIE	An officer will be in touch with you to get your statement as we investigate the accident. We're collecting evidence now, so you won't be able to go to the scene. Best thing for you to do is go home till we get in touch. Do

	you want to tell your mother, or do you want an officer, too?
TIM	I'll tell her. I'll tell her somehow.

FADE OUT:

SCENE VIII

Officer Harper is on duty and hears of the explosion. Knowing those involved tell the captain he would like to be the one who tells his wife.

INT: AFTERNOON AT DEBRA'S HOME

Debra is finishing cleaning up the lunch dishes after putting the girls down for a nap. She hears a loud knock on the door.

FADE IN:

Seeing from the curtains that it's an officer, Debra goes to the door.

DEBRA	Sorry, I wasn't expecting anyone.
OFF. HARPER	Debra I have some bad news for you and the girls.
DEBRA	The judge gave him a slap on the hand, and now he gets to come back in the house he pays for, right?
OFF. HARPER	No, ma'am, he won't be doing that!
DEBRA	So, what's the bad news?

OFF. HARPER	Your husband was involved in an explosion.
DEBRA	How? Where?
OFF. HARPER	On his fishing boat.
DEBRA	His brother fishes with him. Was he in the explosion too.
OFF. HARPER	No, he was on shore about to join him.
DEBRA	Who did this to him?
OFF. HARPER	Do you know something we don't?
DEBRA	No, but he's had no problems with the boat and has had it five years or more now.
OFF. HARPER	Well, Ma'am, he's dead, so he can't cause you any harm, but as his wife, you will need to identify his remains. He had his military dog tags but no ring. He can be identified by some of his tattoos from his military days. There's no need for us to patrol the area now, so you won't be seeing us drive by anymore.
DEBRA	Okay, sir, I'll do that. Just let me call my mother to come sit with the girls.

OFF. HARPER   I'll meet you there in an hour. Bye.

Debra calls her mother and fills her in. Her mother arrives.

BARBARA   What a terrible thing to happen. How are you feeling? Are you okay to drive?

DEBRA   I'm a bit shocked. I feel hurt and relieved all at the same time. I can't believe something like this happened. I feel sad for the girls to grow up without their father but relieved we don't have to deal with any more of his violent actions. The girls don't need to grow up seeing that!

BARBARA   Well, you best be going. We'll talk when you get back.

DEBRA   Don't say anything to the girls till I come home, and we'll tell them together.

FADE OUT:

INT: LATE AFTERNOON.

Officer Harper is waiting outside for Debra. As Debra joins him, they walk in together to identify Joe's body.

FADE IN:

OFF. HARPER   You won't be seeing a whole body intact. You know it was an explosion? Let's identify him first, and then I have a few questions for you.

DEBRA   I understand.

OFF. HARPER   We have parts with tattoos you can identify, his military dog tags, as well as his belongings. You just look at them and tell us if they are Joe's and let us know if anything we have here is not his. Okay!

DEBRA   Yes, sir.

Debra looks in his wallet to see their pictures and begins to cry. His tattoos are still mostly intact, and most of his head remains untouched, but so many parts of his body are broken—shattered beyond recognition.

DEBRA	It's him for sure. I do not see his ring, but he must have taken it off.
OFF. HARPER	Now, let's go talk in the next room.
DEBRA	Help me make sense of this so I can tell the girls in a way their little minds can understand, at least to Susan.
OFF. HARPER	We're investigating it to see if foul play was involved or if this truly was an accident. Can you tell us why he stored gas cans on the boat?
DEBRA	I don't believe he ever done that. I don't think that is allowed. Why?
OFF. HARPER	We found evidence that he had at least two on board. People heard two explosions, and that may have been the second one they heard. Any problems with the engine that you know of?
DEBRA	No, the boat hasn't had a problem since he's had it. I surely would have heard about it if there was. You should know that! However his brother, Tim, would be better able to answer that.
OFF. HARPER	Do you know of anyone who would want to kill him?

DEBRA	What he did to me was all over the papers and T.V., you know.
OFF. HARPER	You got a point there. Well, if we have any more questions, we know where to find you. We'll let you know when his remains will be released for a funeral. If you hear anything, let us know.
DEBRA	Oh my, I have to do that. Okay, let me know. Thanks!

FADE OUT:

SCENE IX

INT: EARLY EVENING.

Debra returns home to see her mom feeding the girls, and they are in pjs, watching cartoons in their bedroom.

BARBARA	Was it truly Joe?
DEBRA	Yes, Mom, no doubt. Now I got to get the strength to tell the girls and do a funeral. I don't know how to do that.
BARBARA	Did Joe have life insurance?
DEBRA	Yes, he got that when he was in the service. Okay, so first, I need to find those papers and contact them.
BARBARA	You'll have to apply for social security for the girls.
DEBRA	What?
BARBARA	Till the girls turn 18 or out of high school, you can get a monthly check to support them.
DEBRA	Really! Oh my, that would help a lot. Ma, will you stay with me till I tell the girls? I'll face the rest tomorrow.

BARBARA	Of, course I will, dear, and you'll have to get a death certificate before you fill for everything else. I'll watch the girls when you do that.
DEBRA	Okay, girls, can you come to the living room for a minute? Daddy's boat had an accident, and Daddy didn't make it. He died and went to heaven.
ALLEY	Good, so he won't come home mad no more and scare me.
DEBRA	Alley, Daddy was in the boat when it blew up.
SUSAN	Did Daddy get hurt like you did and had to go to the hospital for a while like you did?
DEBRA	No, Susan, Daddy died. He won't be coming home anymore.
ALLEY	Well, I don't miss him. He scared me all the time and made my tummy hurt. Can I go watch my cartoons?
DEBRA	Yes, Alley, you may.

Alley runs to her room to watch cartoons.

DEBRA	*(continues)* Susan, do you have any questions?

SUSAN	I'm gonna miss Daddy. He wasn't mad all the time.
DEBRA	No, he wasn't. You were his pride and joy. He loved you a lot, even in the mad times. He just needed help to not be so mad.
SUSAN	Can I have a picture of Daddy on my bedroom wall so I don't forget what he looks like?
DEBRA	You sure can. I'll find one of his pics in his military dress—blues to match your eyes.
SUSAN	Thanks, Mom. I love you!

Susan gives her mom a big hug and goes off to her room.

BARBARA	That went easier than I expected. I'm sure there will be more questions to come in the next few days. I'm proud of how you handled it all. I'll leave you now. Just call me when you need me to watch the girls or just want to talk. Okay?
DEBRA	Thanks for everything, Mom. I'll find that life insurance tonight after the girls go to sleep.

Debra gives her mom a big hug.

BARBARA		I'm sorry you and the girls have to go through this.

DEBRA		Love you, Mom. Bye.

Debra puts the girls to bed and finds the life insurance policy. Then, she heads to the computer in the chatroom.

DEBRA		*(writes)* I'm sure you're all up to speed on all that has happened. The police are questioning in their investigation if it was a planned hit job. Any of you know anything about anyone who may have done this?

The computer is quiet for 3 minutes, making Debra overthink.

DEBRA		*(writes)* Hello! I see over 300 of you are on right now.

A whole bunch of "NOs" come over the screen. Debra shuts the computer down and goes to bed.

INT: THE NEXT MORNING:

The phone rings.

DEBRA Hello?

(silence)

DEBRA What time and where do I pick this up?

Debra grabs a notepad and starts writing.

DEBRA Thank you. I'll take four copies, please.

Debra calls her mom.

BARBARA Hello!

DEBRA Mom, I get to pick up the death certificate today, so I need you to watch the girls. I'll go around and do everything else, so you don't have to keep coming.

BARBARA Okay, dear, but if it gets to be too much, just come home. You can do it another day. I don't mind. I'll be right over; give me a half hour to get myself dressed and over there.

DEBRA	Thanks, Mom.

Debra makes the girls a big breakfast with enough for her mom when she gets there so that Barbara only has to fix the girls some sandwiches for lunch. Barbara arrives at Debra's home.

BARBARA	Hello, dear. Do you have all you need, like the girls' birth certificates and social security cards, as well as yours?
DEBRA	I feel like I'm just going through the motions, doing what I have to do. I believe I have all I need, and I made extra breakfast for you. You can make them a sandwich for lunch. Okay!
BARBARA	We'll make do, dear. Just take it easy and remember, tomorrow's another day. You don't have to do it all today.
DEBRA	I appreciate you, Mom, for being there for me so much right now. Love ya!

INT: LATE AFTERNOON

Debra is off for the day and returns late in the afternoon.

BARBARA	Did you get everything you needed done?
DEBRA	Yes, the funeral is in three days. I'll just need to go shopping to get our dresses for it.
BARBARA	Save that for tomorrow, and we will all go together. You look so tired, dear.
DEBRA	Oh, good, I need to just sit down and process everything.
BARBARA	I wasn't sure when you'd get back, so I made a sandwich for you, too, and the slow cooker has supper going.
DEBRA	Thanks, Mom.
BARBARA	Why don't you have that sandwich and then take a nap yourself? I'll stay here with the girls and go with them in the play yard so the house is quiet for you.
DEBRA	I'll take you up on that one, Mom.

Debra eats and goes to bed. By six o' clock, Barbara allows the girls to wake Debra up for supper, which Barbara has all set up on the table and ready.

SUSAN & ALLEY   Wake up, Mom. It's time for supper, Grandma said.

DEBRA   Oh, girls, what a wonderful way to wake me up—with these two smiling faces.

Debra gives them both a big hug.

SUSAN   Can you smell it, Mom?

DEBRA   Yes, I can. Now, let's get to it.

Debra enters the kitchen and says to her mom.

DEBRA   Why did you let me sleep so long?

BARBARA   You looked like you needed a double nap to get caught up. An officer came while you were sleeping and said he'd drop by tomorrow.

DEBRA   More questions, I suppose. I have plenty myself.

BARBARA   For now, girls, let's eat. I made rolls, too.

They all take their seat, and the girls look at Grandma, who has taken their Dad's seat. Realizing that, Grandma says:

BARBARA   Does anyone want to trade seats?

SUSAN   I will, Grandma.

So they trade seats.

SUSAN   Can we get another bubble bath tonight, Mom?

DEBRA   Do we have any left? If we do, yes; if not, we'll get some more tomorrow.

After supper, the girls take a bath while Debra and her Mom wash dishes.

BARBARA   Susan is old enough and had spent more time with Joe, so she'll be affected more and have more questions as the days go by. Give her time, and it will fade out.

DEBRA   I know, Mom.

BARBARA   I'll get out of your hair now. Know that I'm just a call away, dear.

DEBRA   Bye, Mom, and again, thanks.

Debra gets the girls to bed and gets in the chatroom on the computer.

DEBRA   Hello, everyone.

CAROL   How you doing, girl?

DEBRA   Worn out, confused, and just want to know what happened. Did someone do this where it was all over the news and paper, or was it just an accident somehow?

CAROL   The papers say they are questioning all people at the dock that morning and give a hotline for anyone for tips to be called in. I don't believe anyone would take a father from two little girls.

PAUL   Carol, have you been on top of what Joe put Debra through in front of those two little girls?

DEBRA   True, Paul! In times like this, I tend to look at the girls and not the whole picture. Imagine how much more they would have had to go through in their little lives. The girls could have lost us both, one after the other.

KEVIN   You need now to put this part of your life aside and look toward the future for yourself and your girls. We're all here to hear you out if you need to vent.

DEBRA   Right now, I'm scared of what the future holds and not sure of my judgment in life anymore. Sad for the girls, yet relieved that the fights and blow-ups have come to an end.

PAUL   Debra, you get to start life again. Only keep the best part of the past with you and your girls!

DEBRA   Thanks, Paul. I needed to hear that. I need to get some sleep now and get ready for another day before the funeral. Bye all, and thanks to you all.

FADE OUT:

SCENE X

EXT: AT THE CHURCH'S CEMETERY

Military men are carrying Joe's closed casket to the cemetery from the church next door.

FADE IN:

Debra is walking to the cemetery with her girls and mother when she realizes how many people are there, mostly from the chatroom. A last prayer is being given by Father Burke.

FATHER BURKE Let us bow our heads in prayer.

A basket of cards is given to Debra by the funeral parlor as they begin to leave the cemetery. Debra is stopped by Tom.

TOM   Debra, we in the chatroom ran a GoFundMe for you and the girls. Here is the money that was collected, and we are all here to present it to you in person. If more comes in, we'll bring it to you. It should be enough to support you for a year so you can take your time to get on your feet.

Debra sees the crowd and starts to cry even more, her emotions intensifying beyond all the feelings that were already surging in her.

DEBRA I want to thank you all for this and all the support you have given me and my girls. Please let me hug you all as we leave the cemetery.

FADE OUT:

SCENE XI

INT: HOME AT DEBRA'S HOUSE – NIGHT TIME

The girls have been fed, and Debra is in the living room on the sofa, about to start opening the cards they received at the funeral home.

SUSAN	Mom, can I open some of those cards?
DEBRA	Let's open them together so Mommy can write their names on the envelopes and make sure we send them a thank you card. Okay?

Debra opens the GoFundMe envelope first.

DEBRA	Mom, look at this. It's enough to pay the house off, and still, there would be plenty left for us to live on for a while. I'll have to thank them all again.
BARBARA	There are still good, kind-hearted people in this world. I'll leave you girls to yourself so you can go through those cards. Tomorrow will be the first day of a new life for you and the kids.

THE END

ABOUT THE AUTHOR

Back in 1981, Doris became a certified community advocate, helping her community, from Tiny Todd group leader raising funds to benefit low-income kids and helping low-income families in areas that she was trained in.

In 1984, she received a certificate for her volunteer service from the University Of Maine co-operative service—all about helping kids learn to cook and have proper nutritional values.

Doris then became the treasurer of the Task Force on Human Needs and became a member of the board of directors. She was also the vice president of Maine Association of Independent Neighborhoods, working on pieces of legislation to help the community, as well as the vice president of the American Legion Auxiliary in Lisbon Falls, helping vets and raising funds.

Doris then spent many years doing voluntary work in schools and receiving many awards, starting with Head

Start and then three different schools. She made costumes for plays, published kids' personal classroom books, participated in fluoride treatment for one whole school weekly, and did her favorite classroom crafts. She would do crafts for holidays and weekly crafts on the learned subject of the week to help what they had learned to stick a bit better.

NEWLY PUBLISHED BY AMAZON AND ON KINDLE:

PAWS OF FATE
ISBN: 9798345971840 PAPERBACK
ISBN: 9798345972489 HARDCOVER

OTHER BOOKS PUBLISHED BY THE AUTHOR:

SPLASH OF LOVE
ISBN: 978-1-6655-5808-2 (SC)
ISBN: 978-1-6655-5809-9 (E)

BROKEN HEARTS & SOULS
ISBN: 978-1-6655-6468-7 (SC)
ISBN: 978-1-6655-6469-4 (E)

www.ingramcontent.com/pod-product-compliance
Lightning Source LLC
Chambersburg PA
CBHW041145110526
44590CB00027B/4129